SHAKESPEARE

Mason Crest Publishers, Inc., 370 Reed Road, Broomall, Pennsylvania 19008
866-MCP-BOOK (toll free)

Illustrations copyright
© 2001 Alexander Mikhnushev
Published in association with
Grimm Press Ltd., Taiwan
Printed in Taiwan.

1 3 5 7 9 8 6 4 2

Library of Congress Cataloging-in-
Publication Data:

on file at the Library of Congress.

ISBN 1-59084-157-3
ISBN 1-59084-133-6 (series)

SHAKESPEARE

The Globe Theater Reopened!

"The King of Drama," William Shakespeare, was a partner in the Globe Theater, which was the leading place for performances of his plays. Over the years, these walls have seen audiences weeping during performances of Romeo and Juliet, delighted by jokes in The Comedy of Errors, and terrified by scenes in The Tempest.

Kenny's father was an accountant in a large firm. He joked that he was a human calculator, constantly buried underneath paperwork and accounts. In the evenings, however, he turned into someone quite different; he became an actor. Kenny's father had a dream - that one day he would have the chance to act in one of Shakespeare's plays, for Shakespeare was his idol.

One day, his dream came true.

He was to play the donkey, Bottom, in Shakespeare's play A Midsummer Night's Dream.

Kenny's father was excited - he finally had the chance to show his son what a play was all about. They set off in the morning to the theater for rehearsal,

where Kenny's father murmured his lines and practiced his actions in front of a mirror.

Kenny entertained himself by exploring the theater that was rebuilt according to the original design in the 16th century. It was different from the ordinary modern theater, being circular, made of wood, having a center platform stage, and an open thatched roof. Tonight was opening night, so the magnificent curtain hung behind the stage and the props were pilled high. Curious, Kenny climbed onto the stage, poking and prodding at the unknown objects.

"Ohhhh!" Not noticing the hole in the stage, Kenny took one step into the hole and vanished.

"William! Are you asleep?" John Shakespeare shook his son awake. John was once a farmer, later moving to Stratford as a glove merchant. He made a good living, and money was plentiful. He also bought land and dabbled in politics, eventually becoming the high bailiff of Stratford-on-Avon. That day, John had brought his son to watch the touring acting company set up stage and prepare for their performances. William had dozed off among the activity going on around him.

William opened his eyes to find himself surrounded by a flurry of commotion and costumed characters singing on stage. The audience was mesmerized by the play, laughing and crying out in delight. A sleepy and confused William asked his father, "Where are we? Why am I here?"

"Today is the day the touring company is performing, and we're going to watch the play, remember?" John replied.

"Oh, yes! So we did." William jumped up; he wasn't going to miss it for anything! In their small town, the opportunity to see a play only came during local fairs and festivals.

John lifted William up on his shoulders so he could see clearly.

The plain stage had been transformed magically into a thick forest with the legendary Robin Hood and John Locksley in mid-battle.

William, enthralled at the scene before him, couldn't take his eyes off the stage. It was perhaps the first time he had witnessed such a play, and it marked the beginning of his love for theater.

Stratford is situated upon the beautiful river Avon, and in those days, it was a typical English village. The local populace numbered only a few thousand, most of whom were engaged in farming or small business.

It was in this simple environment that Shakespeare matured and grew into a

great playwright. As a child he would have to perform the same routine each day: unwillingly he would shoulder his satchel and amble at a snail's pace to school. As soon as the bell rang, he'd be off like a shot. He loved to stroll in the forest or along the Avon towpath more than anything else.

At age eleven, William's father sent him to one of the best local schools,

famous for its study of Latin. Studying Latin was like receiving the key to the

mighty door of classical literature. Shakespeare couldn't help but fall in love with poetry, music, and historical stories.

However, bad luck struck the family. John Shakespeare's business suffered

serious financial difficulties, and he had no choice but to sell his land. To avoid his debtors, John couldn't even attend church and was eventually expelled from local government.

"Son, I've got no money left to send you to university. You'll have to stay here to help me look after your brother and sister," said John to his son, knowing there was no alternative.

To help his father, William worked

was a noisy and crowded environment.

"Do I really want to live like this for the rest of my life?" Shakespeare asked himself. The answer was no. He made the decision to leave his wife and children with his father, pass on the business to his younger brother, and set off on his own to try his fortune in London.

hard. He married, had three children, and the now-expanded family lived together under one roof in their old house. It

William fell in love with London the moment he arrived. It was bursting with exquisite churches, cathedrals, palaces, and castles; at the same time, every corner was also filled with vagabonds, vagrants, and criminals. It staged every tragedy and comedy imaginable.

The Elizabethan era saw England become great, and Queen Elizabeth herself loved the theater. She strongly supported the industry, inviting drama groups to perform at the palace. Any

opportunity, festival, and holiday saw theater troupes gather and perform. Under the Queen's patronage, the social status of playwrights and actors improved greatly, and playhouses appeared all over the country, such as The Theater, The Curtain, and The Rose.

This was a good opportunity for a poor man to become famous, and Shakespeare was determined to prove himself under such circumstances. However, his fellow playwrights had already established themselves as famous poets. Did a country boy stand a chance with such competition?

Shakespeare decided to try his luck joining a theater company. In those days, companies consisted of a small group of people, each of whom invested a sum of money in order to buy a script, props, costumes, etc. Once the performances were finished, profits were split according to each person's investment. They also hired a writer, a musician, or actors. Or, they might employ a writer, a musician, and actors to work for the duration of the play.

For example, in a play that had female roles, they would need to employ a young boy to act, since women could not act in those days and the young boy's unbroken voice and hairless face would make acting women's parts possible.

At first, Shakespeare tended the horses and carriages of the wealthier audience members who came to see the plays.

Then he was a prompter (someone who reminds actors of their lines when they forget them). To do this job well, he memorized entire plays so that he could prompt the words at any time, regardless of the role or its lines.

During the course of this repetitive work, Shakespeare discovered his talent for writing plays and understanding of the skills involved, such as structure, plot, timing, and characterization. Soon, the company began using him as an actor.

The life of an actor was hard. In order to keep the audience amused, scripts changed continually, and that meant a lot of memorization for the actors in addition to rehearsals.

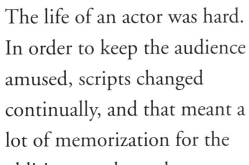

If the cast, venue, or props suddenly changed at the last

minute, one had to improvise. Not an easy feat considering that the script was written like one long poem, with careful attention to rhythm and rhyme. To improvise off the top of one's head without a sense and understanding of literature was almost impossible.

Due to his love for literature, the adaptation of texts fell more and more on Shakespeare's shoulders. Meanwhile, he began writing his own scripts.

To attract audiences, theater companies used every means possible to recruit popular actors, and new scripts appeared every week. Under such circumstances, talented playwrights were highly valuable. They drew inspiration primarily from Greek and Roman mythology and legends, folklore, and tales of fantasy and mysticism.

However, Shakespeare wanted to create a new type of script writing. Although he liked the use of fantasy and magic for plots, he believed that if he used English kings and English history as a backdrop for his plays, audiences would feel connected. Thus, he wrote historical plays, starting with Henry VI.

The release of Henry VI caused a great sensation. People loved the feeling of familiarity with the characters and the elaborate, poetic language. Shakespeare suddenly became London's most popular playwright and received all sorts of social invitations. Due to the

success of Henry VI, Shakespeare was that season's highest-paid scriptwriter.

Shakespeare's success drew jealous attention. Robert Greene, a member of the "University Wits" (a group of highly educated and talented university graduates who wrote plays and poems) wrote with contempt in his book, Greene's Groates-Worth of Wit, that a man of little intellect and education perceived himself a great scriptwriter, "There is an upstart Crow, beautified with our feathers, that with his Tygers

hart wrapt in a Players hyde, supposes he is as well able to bombast out a blank verse as the best of you: and, being an absolute Johannes Factotum, is in his own conceit the only Shake-scene in a country." Although he did not spell out Shakespeare's name in full, everyone knew his meaning, especially with his use of a line said by the Duke of York in Henry VI.

The Doctor!

In 1592, a dreadful outbreak of plague hit London, spreading like wildfire. In less than a week, more than thousand people died. Corpses lay piled up on carts in every street, and to avoid spreading the disease further, orders came for doors to close in every industry, including London's theaters.

With the theaters closed, troupes had nowhere to stage performances and faced bankruptcy. Some companies dispersed, others relied on the publishing industry; some sold their props, and others had no choice but to leave London.

Shakespeare persevered and used the time to write new plays and develop his poetry. He wrote the long poems Venus and Adonis and The Rape of Lucrece, which he dedicated to the

Earl of Southampton, his patron.

After publication of his poems, Shakespeare received more acclaim, resulting in reprints of his work. Already famed for his acting and scriptwriting, he was now an esteemed poet.

In 1594, the plague situation improved, and the theaters were reopened. Shakespeare became a partner in the theater company, Lord Chamberlain's Men. So long as everyone worked hard to bring in large audiences, each investor would benefit from the profits.

Shakespeare worked hard, writing at least two plays a year, as well as acting in leading roles. Philip Henslowe, manager of the Admiral's Men theater group (a rival theater group) sought every means possible to cause the downfall of the Lord Chamberlain's Men.

the family to display its coat-of-arms, and Shakespeare purchased New Place, one of Stratford's grandest houses.

After his son's death, Shakespeare's writing style changed. He wrote the historical play King Lear, followed by the comedy A Midsummer Night's Dream and then the lovers' tragedy Romeo and Juliet and the satirical The Merchant of Venice.

Shakespeare was producing one successful play after another. Then life dealt a blow - Shakespeare's son, Hamnet, passed away at age 11. The death of his only son deeply affected the writer, as is reflected in his later plays.

Shakespeare was now earning a good living, becoming a relatively wealthy man. In 1596, permission was granted allowing

Despite wide success, the Lord Chamberlain's Men still suffered setbacks, such as when the Lord Chamberlain died. The new Lord Chamberlain, William Brook, seventh Lord Cobham, had little sympathy for the struggle of London's theater groups and was partially responsible in the closure of the city's inn-theaters, leaving Shakespeare's company to search for a new venue. (They later moved into the Swan in 1596).

Shakespeare could not resist making fun of Cobham, and he created a fat and weak warrior in his play Henry IV, naming him "Sir John Oldcastle," after an ancestor of the Cobham family. However, after Cobham's protestations at court, Shakespeare was forced to change the name to the similar-sounding "John Falstaff."

In order to attract a constant audience, the Lord Chamberlain's Men yearned for a theater of their own.

On the night of December 26, a flock of supporters dissembled the old Theater and carried the timbers across the frozen Thames

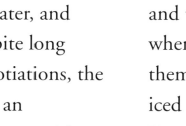

A good opportunity arose when the land lease where Burbage's The Theater - one of London's earliest play venues - stood was due to expire.

River to the opposite bank, where the Burbages had leased land in order to build a new theater.

Shakespeare cheered everyone on, directing the way for those carrying the large beams and timbers, or when they rolled them across the

James Burbage had built The Theater, and despite long negotiations, the landlord failed to come to an

iced river. Shakespeare's rival, Henslowe, could hardly recover from the shock of what the Lord

agreement with James' sons, Richard and Cuthbert Burbage,

Chamberlain's Men and their friends did, especially as the new theater

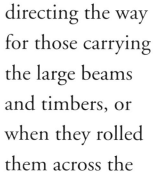

who had inherited the building. They came up with a cunning plan to overcome the problem - although the lease was about to end,

the house itself did not belong to the landowner.

stood just across from his own Rose theater and posed a serious threat to

Henslowe's business.

On performance days, the theater would raise a flag so that all of London would know. The balcony on the second floor allowed for excellent viewing of the play. The third floor (above the stage) called the "Heavens" accommodated

props and also allowed for the miraculous appearance of angels, while below, a trapdoor existed known as "Hell," and was likewise used for symbolic appearances and disappearances.

The ground floor had no seats and provided the cheapest option for the common man to watch a play. In those days, the audience would make their opinion regarding the quality of the play obvious, throwing food at the actors if they didn't like what they saw.

The year 1599 saw the opening of the new playhouse, with Henry V staged as the first play. This magnificent historical play created a great reputation for the new theater. From then on, Shakespeare staged more and more of his plays, gradually casting aside his acting career for that of playwright.

As the plays of Shakespeare received more popularity, problems began to surface regarding illegal publications - in some cases, due to certain actors memorizing an entire play and then repeating it to a publisher for printing. The phenomenon angered Shakespeare, yet he could do nothing to change the situation.

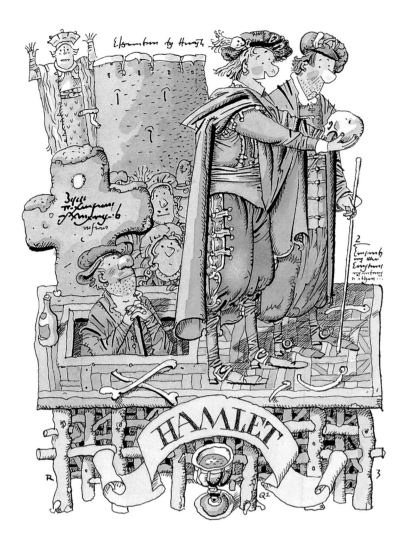

At the time when the Globe and other theaters of London flourished with plays and popularity, politics, with its associated traitors and plotters, suddenly descended upon the theatrical world.

One day, several men came to offer the Lord Chamberlain's Men forty shillings to restage Richard II, one of Shakespeare's early plays, that depicts the unfit King Richard II and the honorable and noble character Bolingbroke, who later became Henry IV.

Unknown to the Lord Chamberlain's Men, this restaging of Richard II was aimed at creating popular support for a traitorous plot against Queen Elizabeth conceived by the Earl of Essex and Shakespeare's patron, the Earl of Southampton. The rebellion failed, Essex was beheaded, and Southampton was imprisoned in the Tower of London.

Fortunately, Shakespeare's company remained unharmed, with no proof of their involvement in the rebellion ever found. Not long afterwards, in 1603, Elizabeth II passed away.

Having weathered this storm, Shakespeare's writings once again took on a new and different tone. He began to research the motivation and drive behind human relationships, generosity and selfishness, power, fate, and corruption. It led to the following four tragedies: Hamlet, Othello, King Lear, and Macbeth. Each leading character, whether the proud Lear, vengeful Hamlet, or jealous Othello, faces catastrophe; all are unable to foresee the cataclysmic consequences his innate character temperament binds him to. The plays marked the climax of Shakespeare's career.

KING LEAR

MACBETH

After the death of Queen Elizabeth II, James I supported the Lord Chamberlain's Men, and they changed their name to the King's Men. They didn't receive much money from him, but they were honored that he enjoyed their plays.

In 1608, they moved their winter performances to the indoor theater James Burbage had built in Blackfriars. The new theater provided shelter for the

company during the winter months; no longer did they have to endure exposure to England's harsh weather. Around this time, the plague appeared again in London, with frequent closures of the theaters as before. Shakespeare used these times to return home to Stratford and write new plays. However,

traveling back and forth took its toll. At age 46, he thought perhaps the time had come to stay home.

In 1610, he left London for Stratford, but he kept writing, for he still burst with ideas for new plays. He wrote The Winter's Tale, The Tempest, and other works co-written with

different playwrights.

In 1613, the Globe staged Henry VIII. During the play, a salute of guns was to be fired for the arrival of Henry VIII, and during a performance, the thatched roofing caught fire, setting the entire theater ablaze and completely destroying the Globe. Fortunately, the audience and Shakespeare's scripts escaped unharmed.

Shakespeare led a comfortable life in his later years in Stratford. His eldest daughter had married, and he lived with his wife and younger daughter in New Place. His neighbors and the local people of Stratford, who all respected and admired him, held him in great esteem.

He had planned to publish his plays himself, since many he wrote never saw publication and others that were published contained mistakes. In fact, he frequently corrected and altered parts of plays that he believed were not up to his standards.

Unfortunately, Shakespeare never lived to see the full publication of his works. Not long after his younger daughter married, he caught fever and died on April 23, 1616.

"Wake up! Wake up!"

Little Kenny felt someone shaking him.

"Leave me alone." He opened his sleepy eyes to find himself face to face with a donkey.

Kenny jumped in fright and started to cry.

"Don't cry! It's only me! You were dreaming!" Kenny's father said softly.

Kenny looked about. The stage had been set, and he found himself in a midsummer night's forest, surrounded by elves and fairies.

"Where am I?" Kenny thought he had already woken up. Had he suddenly fallen into another dream? He pinched himself to make sure he was indeed awake.

The summer nights are many and long!

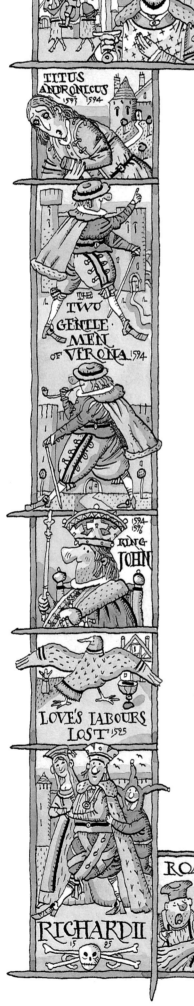

A CHRONOLOGY OF SHAKESPEARE'S WORKS

THE PLAYS

1589–90	Henry VI, Part 1
1590–91	Henry VI, Part 2
1590–91	Henry VI, Part 3
1592–93	Richard III
1592–94	The Comedy of Errors
1593–94	Titus Andronicus
1593–94	The Taming of the Shrew
1594	The Two Gentlemen of Verona
1594–95	Love's Labor's Lost
1594–96	King John
1595	Richard II
1595–96	Romeo and Juliet
1595–96	A Midsummer Night's Dream
1596–97	The Merchant of Venice
1596–97	Henry IV, Part I
1597	The Merry Wives of Windsor
1598	Henry IV, Part II
1598–99	Much Ado About Nothing
1599	As You Like It
1599	Henry V
1599	Julius Caesar
1600–01	Hamlet
1600–01	Twelfth Night
1601–02	Troilus and Cressida

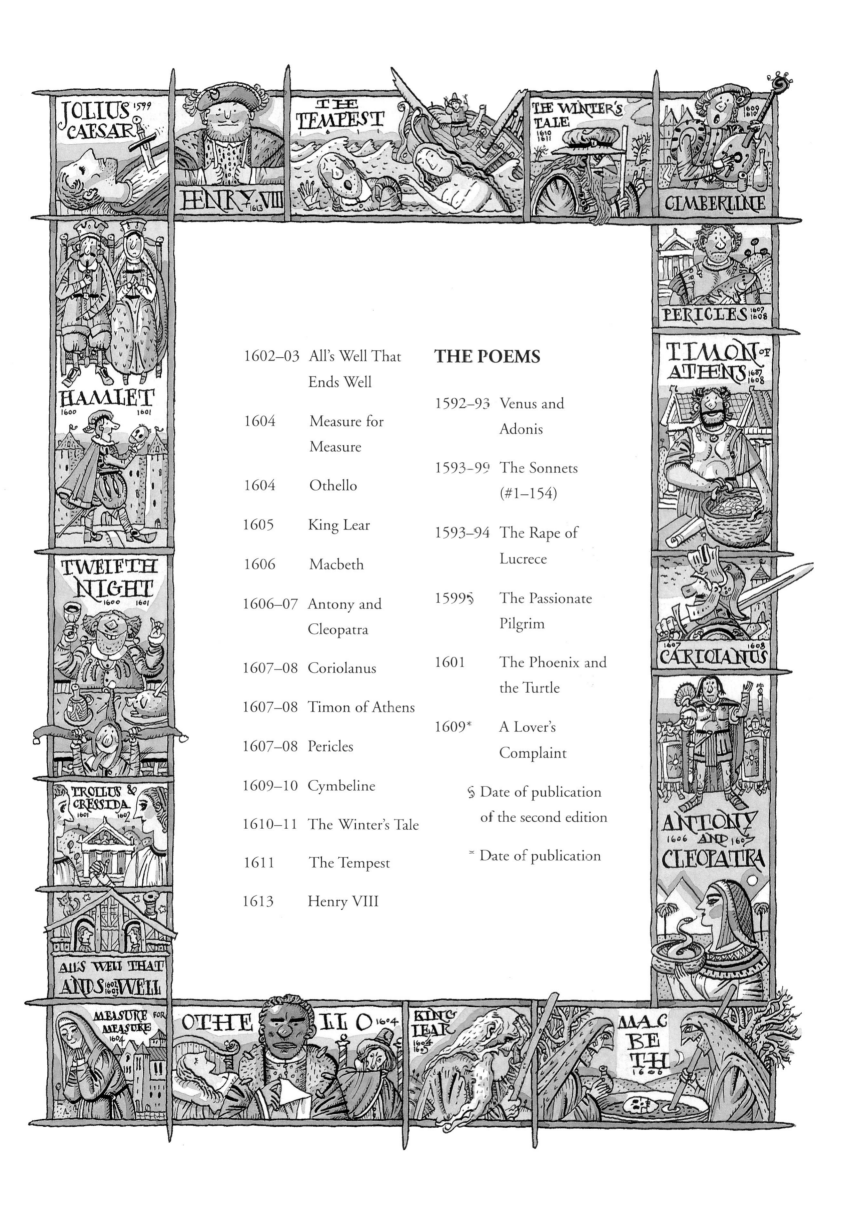

1602–03 All's Well That
         Ends Well

1604   Measure for
         Measure

1604   Othello

1605   King Lear

1606   Macbeth

1606–07 Antony and
         Cleopatra

1607–08 Coriolanus

1607–08 Timon of Athens

1607–08 Pericles

1609–10 Cymbeline

1610–11 The Winter's Tale

1611   The Tempest

1613   Henry VIII

THE POEMS

1592–93 Venus and
         Adonis

1593–99 The Sonnets
         (#1–154)

1593–94 The Rape of
         Lucrece

1599§   The Passionate
         Pilgrim

1601   The Phoenix and
         the Turtle

1609*   A Lover's
         Complaint

§ Date of publication
  of the second edition

* Date of publication